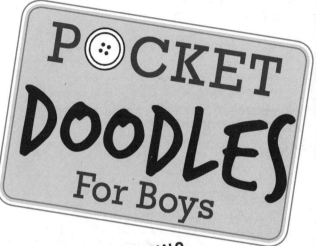

POCKET DOODLES For Boys

CHRIS SABATINO

GIBBS SMITH
TO ENRICH AND INSPIRE HUMANKIND
Salt Lake City | Charleston | Santa Fe | Santa Barbara

First Edition
14 13 12   10

Text and illustrations © 2010 Chris Sabatino

Published by
Gibbs Smith
P.O. Box 667
Layton, Utah 84041

1.800.835.4993 orders
www.gibbs-smith.com

Manufactured in Manitoba, Canada in February 2012
by Friesens
Job #72160

Gibbs Smith books are printed on either recycled,
100% post-consumer waste, FSC-certified papers or
on paper produced from a 100% certified sustainable
forest/controlled wood source.

ISBN 13: 978-1-4236-0756-4
ISBN 10: 1-4236-0756-2

WELCOME!

This book is full of fun and bizarre ideas that I hope will inspire you to doodle. You don't have to draw what the book asks you to draw. Draw what you like—there are no rules here. This is *your* adventure!

Thanks to my wife, kids & friends, who inspired many ideas in this book, and special thanks to my editor, Jared Smith, a very cool guy to talk, create & laugh with.

CHRIS SABATINO

(The weird guy who wrote & drew this book.)

Disclaimer: This book will not make you an artist . . . because you already are one!

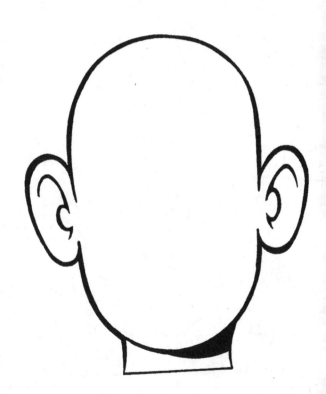

START:

DRAW YOUR FACE (AND HAIR)
ON THE FIRST DAY OF SCHOOL!

SNICKER DOODLE:

EVERYONE iS LAUGHiNG AT SOMETHING. DRAW iT!

SCARY DOODLE:

EVERYONE iS AFRAID OF SOMETHING. DRAW iT!

BURGER:

DRAW THE MOST AWESOME BURGER EVER!

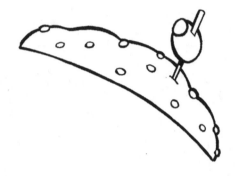

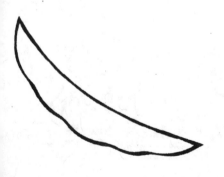

FRIES:

GIVE EACH FRENCH FRY A FACE
BEFORE YOU EAT THEM!

SMALL FRIES

JOHNNY ATE HiS MOTHER'S LEFTOVER SPAGHETTI DiNNER:
DRAW HIS VOMIT!
(meatballs optional)

BiLLY ATE THE CAFETERiA'S MYSTERY MEAT SURPRiSE:

DRAW HiS VOMiT!

(include meaty chunks)

DRAW LOW:

DRAW THE BOTTOM HALF OF THIS ALIEN!

DRAW HIGH:

DRAW THE TOP HALF OF THIS ROBOT!

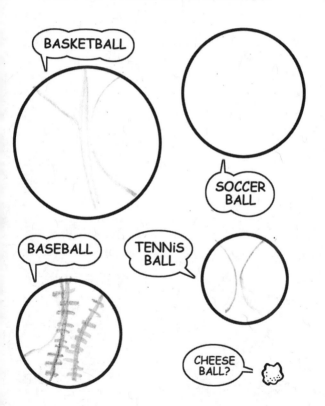

SPIT BALLS:

DRAW THE WET & WILD SPITBALLS
FLYING ABOUT IN THIS SPITBALL BATTLE!

HEAVY METAL:

WHAT'S THIS GIANT MAGNET HOLDING UP?

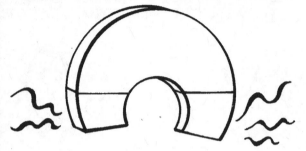

HANG MAN:

WHAT'S THIS MAN HANGING ONTO?

OH, YES!

DRAW THE BEST BiRTHDAY PRESENT YOU'VE EVER RECEiVED!

OH, NO!

DRAW THE WORST BiRTHDAY PRESENT YOU'VE EVER GOTTEN!

NUCLEAR FAMILY:

THIS iS ADAM the ATOM.
DRAW HiS FAMiLY!

CELL-EBRITY:

TURN THiS LiViNG CELL iNTO A MOViE STAR.
GiVE iT A FACE, LiMBS AND SUNGLASSES
(and don't forget a cell phone)!

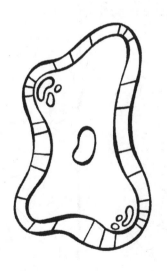

JACK-O-DOODLE:

DECORATE THiS
JACK-O-LANTERN!

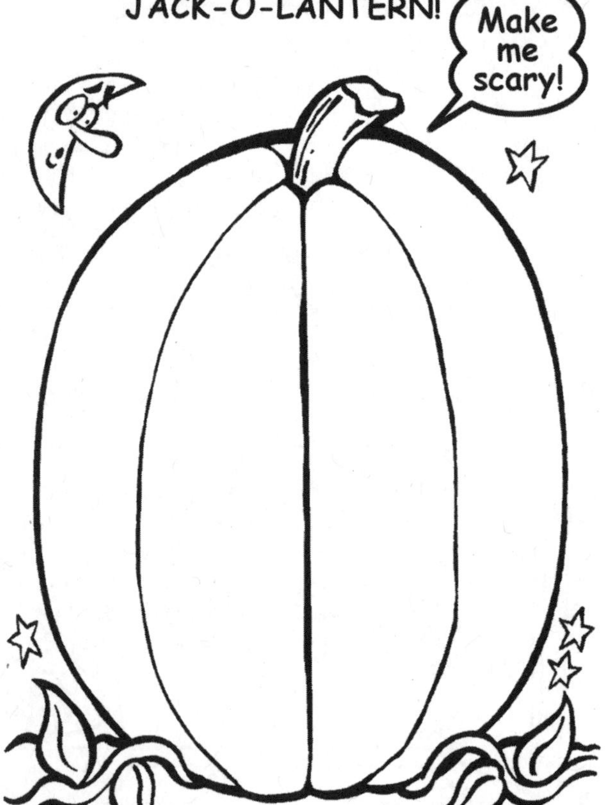

DOODLE-O-WEEN:
DRAW THE WEIRDEST TRICK-OR-TREATER EVER!

COMIC ARTIST:

DRAW PICTURES TO FIT THE WORDS!

DRAW YOUR FAMILY MEMBERS

FAMILY RIDE:

DRAW THE COOLEST VEHiCLE
THAT'S PERFECT FOR YOUR FAMiLY
(no station wagons)!

SWINE FLEW:

DRAW THE REST OF THIS FLYING PIG!

OCTO-ART:

DRAW THE ARMS ON THIS OCTOPUS ARTIST AND CREATE HiS ARTWORK!

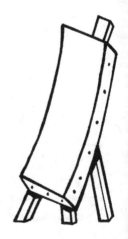

ABRACA-DOODLE:

THE MAGICIAN TRIED TO PULL A RABBIT OUT OF HIS HAT, BUT SOMETHING SCARY APPEARED INSTEAD! DRAW IT!

HARRY POOPER:

THiS YOUNG WiZARD FELL ASLEEP ON THE MOON. DRAW THE MOON!

TACKLE-A-TOON:

DESIGN A COOL TEAM LOGO
FOR THIS FOOTBALL HELMET!

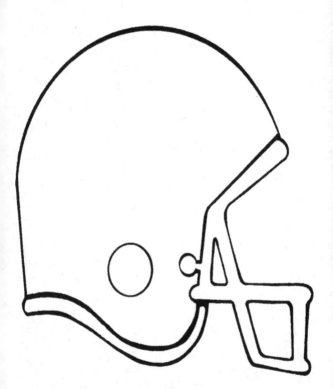

SUPER SANTA:

DRAW SANTA CLAUS AS A SUPERHERO!
(Don't forget his rocket-launcher boots: Missile Toes)

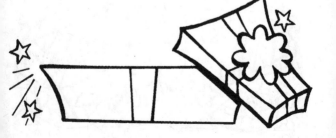

BASKETCASE:

DRAW THE EASTER BUNNY AS A SUPERVILLAIN (with a rotten-egg bazooka)!

HOLI-DAZE:

ILLUSTRATE AN EPIC BATTLE BETWEEN SUPER SANTA & THE BASKETCASE BUNNY!

DREAMS:

DRAW WHAT THIS KID IS DREAMING ABOUT!

SCHEMES:

DRAW THIS KID'S NIGHTMARE!

SPACESHIP:

DESIGN A COOL SPACESHIP
FOR YOU TO PILOT!

SPACE STATION:

DESIGN AN AWESOME SPACE STATION
WHERE YOU CAN PARK YOUR SHIP!

YOU RULE:

YOU RECEIVED A TROPHY BECAUSE YOU'RE GREAT AT SOMETHING. DRAW THE TOP OF THE TROPHY AND FILL OUT THE PLATE!

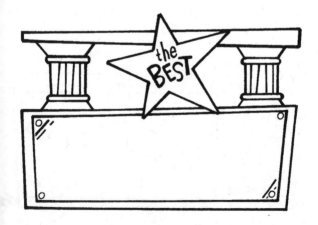

YOU ROCK:

YOUR TOWN DEDICATED A
STATUE TO YOU. DRAW THE STATUE
AND FILL OUT THE PLAQUE!

SNOW WARS:

YOU'RE UNDER ATTACK!
DRAW A SNOW FORT, FAST!

SNOW SHOCK:

DRAW WHAT THE FLiPPED-OUT RiDER iS ABOUT TO SLED iNTO!

CAREER CHANGE:
TURN THIS BORING BUSINESSMAN INTO A CRAZY PIRATE!

WICKED MAKEOVER:

TURN THiS BEAUTY QUEEN iNTO A SCARY WiTCH!

BOXERS:

DRAW THE PERSON WHO iS KNOCKiNG OUT THE CHAMP!

ROCK:

DRAW YOURSELF AND YOUR FRIENDS IN THIS BAND!

STARS:

YOUR BAND RECORDED AN AWESOME
CD. DESIGN THE CD COVER!

SCHOOL DAZE:

THE CAFETERIA LADY MADE YOUR FAVORITE LUNCH. DRAW IT!

SCHOOL HAZE:

THE GYM TEACHER iS LETTiNG YOU DO YOUR FAVORiTE ACTiViTY DURiNG GYM. DRAW iT!

HORSING AROUND:

A CENTAUR IS HALF MAN AND HALF HORSE. DRAW THE HORSE PART!

SOMETHING'S FISHY:

DRAW THE FIN ON THIS FRIENDLY MERMAID!

STICK IT!

BILLY iS BiZARRE.
HE'S USiNG SOMETHiNG WEiRD AS A
HOCKEY STiCK. DRAW iT!

FIRE:

GIVE THE SUN SOME CHARACTER: MAKE HiM THE RED-HOT GUARDIAN OF THE SKY!

ICE:

GIVE THIS SNOWMAN
SOME PERSONALITY: MAKE HIM
AN ICE-COLD WARRIOR!

FIERY FREEZE:

DRAW A BATTLE BETWEEN THE SUN AND THE SNOWMAN!

PICK YOUR NOSE:

PICK THE NOSE MOST LiKE YOURS AND DRAW YOUR FACE AROUND iT!

PICK YOUR SCAB:

SKATEBOARD ACCIDENT! GROSSEST
SCAB ON KNEE EVER! DRAW iT!

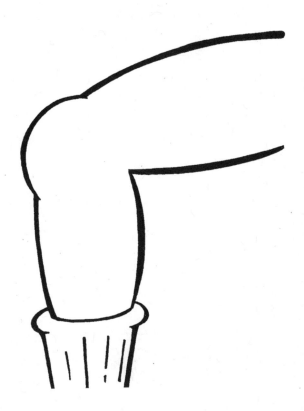

OUTER SPACE:

DRAW WHAT'S OUTSIDE THE SPACESHIP'S WINDOW!

UNDER SEA:
DRAW WHAT'S OUTSIDE THE SUBMARINE'S WINDOW!

FAMILY TREE:

TURN THE HEADS ON THIS FAMILY
TREE INTO YOUR FAMILY MEMBERS!

FAMILY HOME:

DRAW YOUR HOUSE OR THE BUILDING YOU LIVE IN INSIDE THIS SNOW GLOBE!

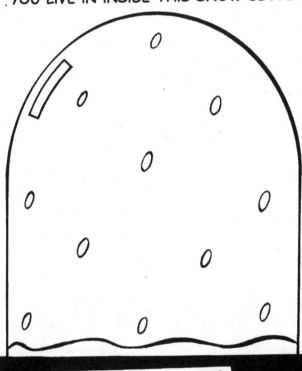

HOME

FERTILIZED:

YOUR PLANT HAS GROWN INTO A
HUNGRY, KID-EATING MONSTER!
DRAW IT!

FLUSHED:

SOMEONE FLUSHED A GOLDFISH DOWN THE TOILET. NOW iT'S BACK, MUTATED AND READY TO TAKE REVENGE ON ALL HUMANS. DRAW iT!

BY LAND:

DRAW SOMEONE YOU WOULDN'T
EXPECT ON THIS SKATEBOARD!

BY SEA:

YOUR SURFBOARD HAS BEEN STOLEN
BY A SEA MONSTER. DRAW IT!

FROM ABOVE:

DRAW WHAT THIS GUY IS DROPPING FROM THE HELICOPTER!

HAIRY:

TURN THIS MOUSE INTO A WEREWOLF!

SCARY:

DRAW WiNGS ON THiS NUTTY BAT!

DRAW-A-BUS:
DRAW THE SCHOOL BUS DRIVER!

FILL-A-BUS:

FILL THIS BUS WITH RIDERS!

THE ART OF EMOTIONS:

FEAR

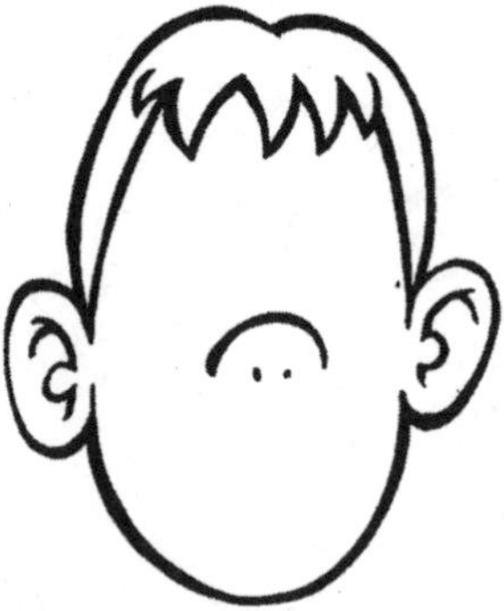

HAPPiNESS

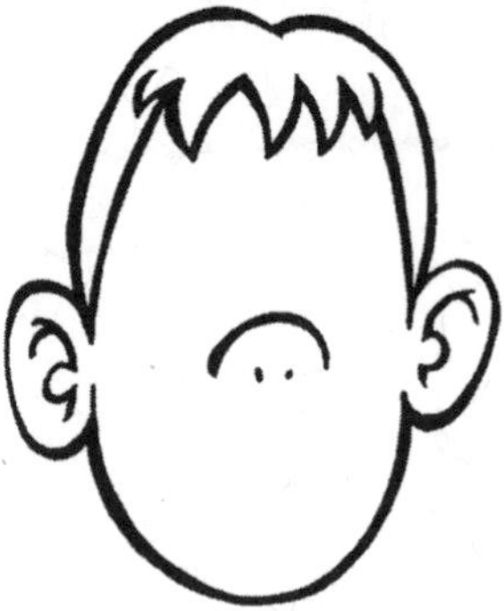

PRiDE

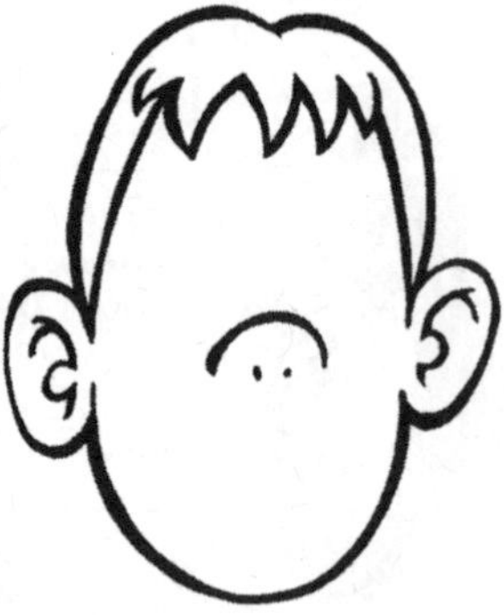

SADNESS

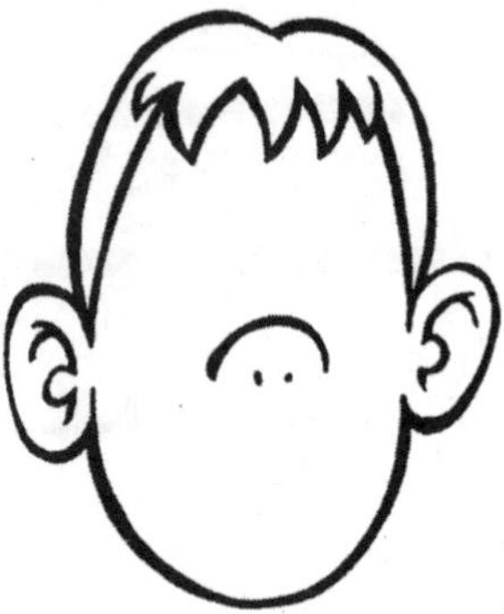

ART EXPRESSES EMOTIONS. DRAW THE EMOTIONS ON THE FACES BELOW!

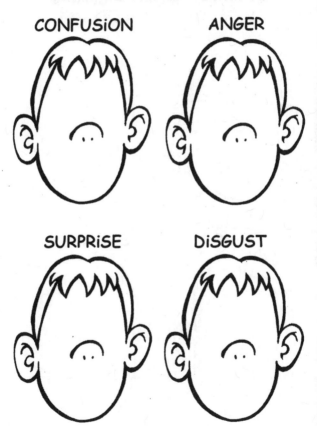

MUMMY:

DRAW THE MUMMY COMING OUT OF THIS SARCOPHAGUS!

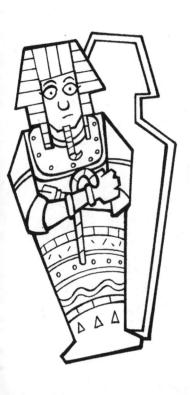

DADDY:

DRAW THIS DADDY LONGLEGS
WEARING 8 DIFFERENT SHOES!

GAS IN A GLASS:

YOU'VE CAPTURED THE WORLD'S FIRST FART BUG AND PUT IT IN A JAR. DRAW THE FART BUG!

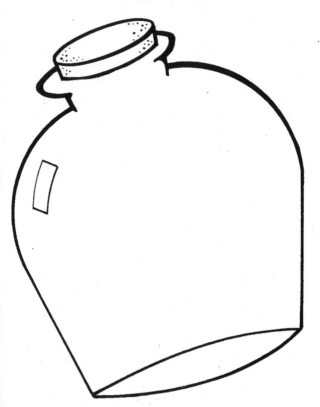

GAS IN A CAN:

DESIGN A LABEL FOR THIS CAN OF BEANS FEATURING YOUR FAVORITE GASSY PERSON!

FOOD FIGHT:

DRAW A FOOD FIGHT BETWEEN
YOUR FAVORITE FOOD AND THE
FOOD YOU HATE THE MOST!

FIGHT FOOD:

DRAW YOURSELF BATTLING THIS SWASHBUCKLING SQUASH!

CAPTURE:

YOU'VE CAPTURED A COOTIE.
DRAW WHAT iT LOOKS LiKE UP CLOSE!

CEREAL:

CREATE AN AWESOME BREAKFAST CEREAL AND DESIGN THE BOX!

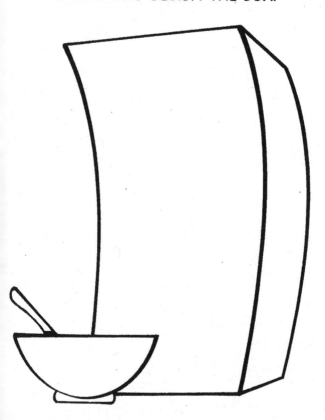

MILK:

DRAW A COW.

WELCOME TO THE DOODLE ZOO:

DRAW WHAT EVERYONE IN THE DOODLE ZOO NEEDS!

ACTION:

DRAW A MOVIE SCENE!

RE-ACTION:

DRAW WHAT'S MAKING THIS
WHEELCHAIR GO SO FAST!

NEW INVENTION: 1

DRAW A CELL PHONE THAT INCLUDES A NOSE PICKER AND A GUMBALL MACHINE.

NEW INVENTION: 2

DRAW A PENCIL THAT WILL DO
YOUR HOMEWORK FOR YOU!

RE-DO:
REDRAW THIS LIBRARIAN AS A FUNNY CLOWN!

RE-DOODLE:
REDRAW THiS CHEF AS AN ADVENTUROUS ASTRONAUT!

BIG PLANT:

JACK BOUGHT SOME MAGIC BEANS
THAT GREW iNTO A BEANSTALK.
DRAW THE BEANSTALK!

BIG PROBLEM:

UP THE BEANSTALK, JACK WAS GRABBED BY AN ANGRY GIANT. DRAW THE GIANT!

DRAW RIGHT:

DRAW THE RIGHT SIDE OF THIS ROCK MONSTER!

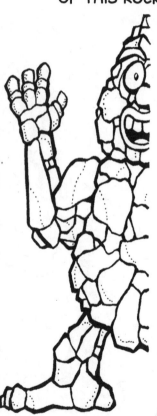

DRAW LEFT:

DRAW THE LEFT SiDE OF THiS SLiME MONSTER!

SLICES ONE:

DRAW YOUR FAVORITE TOPPINGS ON THESE PIZZA SLICES!

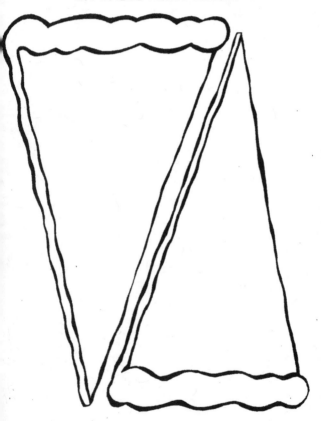

SLICES TWO:

DRAW YOUR FAVORITE SANDWICH
BETWEEN THESE TWO SLICES OF BREAD!

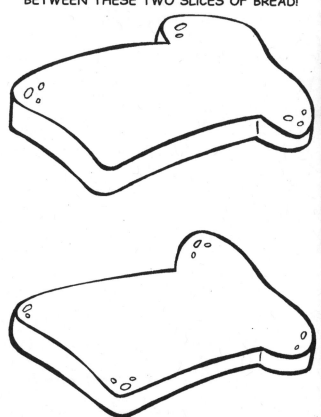

YES, THERE IS A GHOST IN
YOUR CLOSET. DRAW IT!

SHOO!

THERE'S SOMETHING STRANGE OUTSIDE YOUR BEDROOM WINDOW. DRAW IT!

STUCK:

YOUR FRIEND iS STUCK iN
A GiANT SPiDERWEB. DRAW iT!

YUCK:

NOW DRAW THE GiANT UGLY SPiDER
THAT iS ABOUT TO EAT YOUR FRiEND!

POOP-O-RAMA:

DRAW THE POOP THAT
GOES WITH EACH DOG!

PUKE-O-RAMA:

DRAW THE HAIR BALLS BEING COUGHED UP BY THIS CAT!

MOVING UP:

DESIGN A FUTURISTIC CITY ON THE CLOUDS WHERE YOU'D LIKE TO LIVE SOMEDAY!

GOING DOWN:

DESIGN AN UNDERWATER RESORT WHERE YOU'D LIKE TO VACATION SOMEDAY!

FOOD FUN:

THE PINEAPPLE IS THROWING A BASH IN THE FRIDGE. DRAW HIS GUESTS!

CONNECT THE DOT:

DUMMY DOT ATE CLAY AND iT MADE
HER ARMS, LEGS AND NECK LiKE PUTTY.
DRAW THEM!

CONNECT THE DUDES:
DRAW THESE GUYS SOME BODIES!

BUGGED:

THE MAD SCIENTIST CREATED A NEW GIANT MONSTER INSECT. DRAW IT!

SWATTED:
DRAW THE GIANT MONSTER INSECT SQUASHED!

CRAZY DRAW:

DRAW AN ELECTRIC MARSHMALLOW-
EATING DOGFISH WITH TENTACLES
PLAYING THE GUITAR!

CRAZIER DRAW:

DRAW A VAMPIRE BiRTHDAY CAKE
WiTH SiX LEGS PLAYiNG HOCKEY!

EGG-UCATOR:
YOUR TEACHER LAID AN EGG.
DRAW WHAT HATCHED!

EGG HEAD:
DRAW THIS PRINCIPAL'S BRAIN!

DOODLE MOUNTAIN:

DRAW YOURSELF OR SOMEONE iMPORTANT
TO YOU ON MOUNT RUSHMORE!

MOUNT RUSHMORE

LAVA MOUNTAIN:

MAKE THIS VOLCANO ERUPT. DRAW
THE SMOKE, FLAMES AND LAVA!

PET UPSET:
DRAW THE PET YOUR PARENTS WILL NEVER LET YOU HAVE!

SITTER IN CRITTER:

DRAW THE NEW SHAPE OF YOUR SNAKE
AFTER iT SWALLOWS THE BABYSiTTER
(you didn't need a sitter anyway)!

A MACHINE FOR TIME:

DESIGN A COOL NEW CONTRAPTION TO TELL THE TIME!

THE JOKER:

DRAW A FUNNY PERSON iN YOUR LiFE
AS THE JOKER ON THiS PLAYiNG CARD!

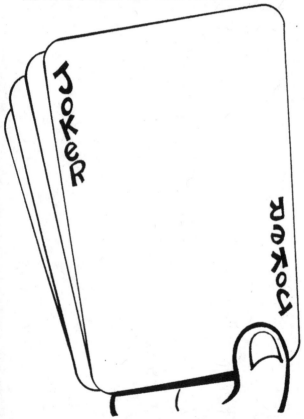

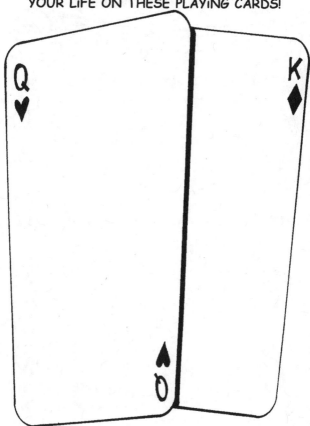

CARTOON SAFARI:

DRAW WHAT YOU SEE IN THE JUNGLE!

TOTEM TOON:

DRAW YOUR FACE AND THE FACES OF YOUR FRIENDS ON THIS TOTEM POLE!

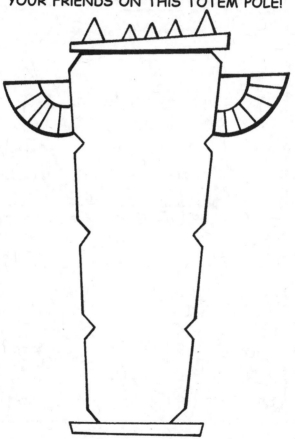

COMIC WRITER:

FiLL iN THE WORD BALLOONS!

FREAKY FOOD:

THE MAD SCIENTIST BROUGHT THIS CARROT TO LIFE. GIVE IT A FACE AND OUTFIT!

DOLL-HEAD SOUP:

YOU'VE COLLECTED ALL THE BARBIE HEADS
IN YOUR TOWN & MADE THEM iNTO SOUP.
DRAW THE SOUP, YOU WEiRDO!

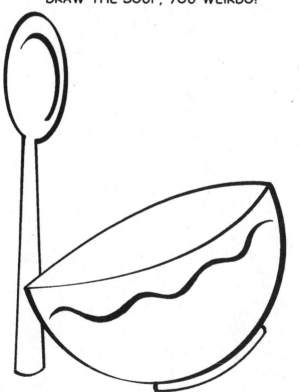

BAD DAY:

DRAW THE ONE THING THAT ALWAYS RUINS YOUR DAY!

WORSE DAY:
DRAW THE WORST WEATHER DAY EVER. INCLUDE RAIN, LiGHTNiNG, HAiL, WiND, SNOW AND MORE!

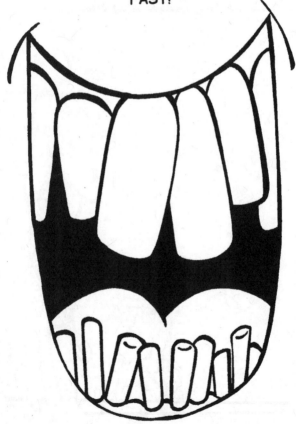

X-TOON:
YOUR DOCTOR TOOK YOUR X-RAY.
DRAW iT!

MY SPACE:

DRAW WHATEVER YOU LIKE ON THIS PAGE!

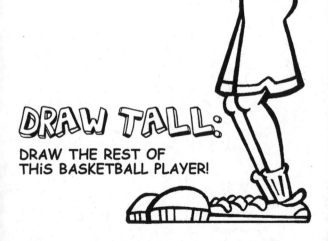

DRAW TALL:

DRAW THE REST OF
THIS BASKETBALL PLAYER!

DRAW SHORT:

DRAW THE REST OF THIS LEPRECHAUN AND FILL UP HIS POT OF GOLD!

STAGE FRIGHT:

IT'S YOUR FIRST TIME ONSTAGE.
DRAW YOUR PERFORMANCE!

AUDIENCE FRIGHT:

DRAW THE REACTION OF THE AUDIENCE TO YOUR UNIQUE PERFORMANCE!

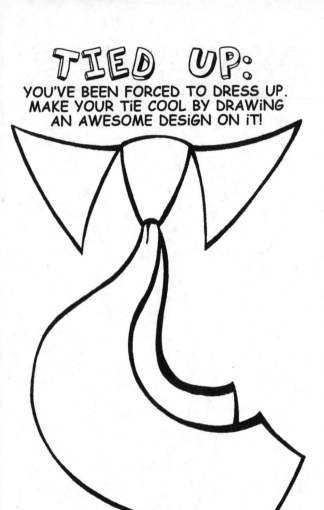

KEEP OFF!

DO NOT DRAW ON THIS PAGE AT
ALL OR YOU ARE IN BIG TROUBLE!
I MEAN IT!

DON'T EVEN THINK ABOUT IT, YOUNG MAN!

MIRROR ART:
DRAW THIS KID'S MANY REFLECTIONS IN THIS HOUSE OF MIRRORS!

MUTT TOON:

DRAW THIS CHIHUAHUA'S PET BOY!

WIZARD OF TOONZ

DRAW THE HEADS OF YOUR FRIENDS THAT MATCH THE CHARACTERS' PERSONALITIES!

FLYING MONKEY:

YOU ARE A FLYING MONKEY. DRAW YOUR
MONKEY HEAD AND YOUR FLYING WINGS!

KANGAROO:

THERE WAS A MIX-UP AT THE ZOO,
DRAW THE SURPRISING ANIMAL THAT'S
IN THE KANGAROO'S POUCH!

BUCKAROO:
DRAW YOUR FAVORITE PRESIDENT OR SOMEONE YOU KNOW ON THIS THREE-DOLLAR BILL!

SICK SUNDAE:

COVER THIS ICE CREAM SUNDAE WITH SCABS, BOOGERS, DANDRUFF, WORMS AND OTHER GROSS STUFF!

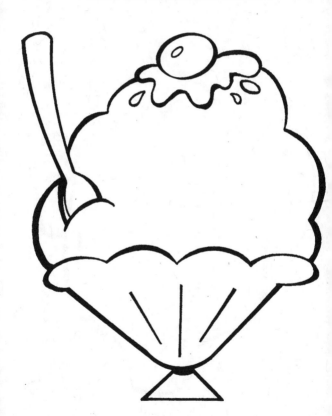

FUTURE DUDE:
DRAW A COOL TIME MACHINE!

CAVE KID:

DRAW YOURSELF AS A PREHISTORIC CAVEMAN!

KA-BOOM:

THIS CLOWN'S CANNON SHOOTS
SOMETHING FUNNY. DRAW IT!

OOPS:

DRAW THE BiZARRE OBJECTS THiS PERFORMER iS JUGGLiNG!

STRANDED:

DRAW THE ONE THING YOU WOULD
WANT TO HAVE IF YOU WERE
STRANDED ON A DESERTED ISLAND
(besides this book)!

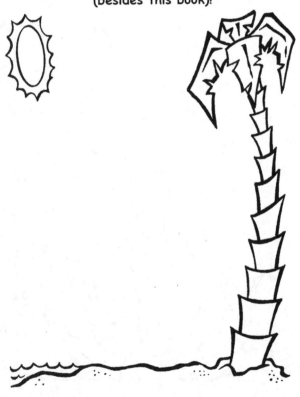

SEA-MAIL:

WHILE ON THE ISLAND, YOU CAN SEND MESSAGES IN BOTTLES. WHAT WOULD YOU WRITE, AND TO WHOM?

MR. MONSTER:
DRAW FRANKENSTEIN'S BABY!

MS. MONSTER:

MEDUSA IS A MONSTER WITH SNAKES FOR HAIR. DRAW HER FRIGHTENING HAIRDO!

DRAW LIGHT:

DRAW WHAT'S iN THE BACKYARD!

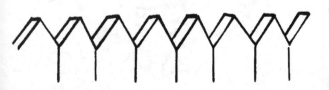

DRAW DARK:
DRAW WHAT'S IN THE ATTIC!

STRONG:

DRAW THE WEIGHT LIFTER!

SMOOTH:
DRAW THE SAXOPHONE PLAYER!

YOU.S.A.

**YOU'VE STARTED YOUR OWN COUNTRY.
DRAW YOUR FLAG!**

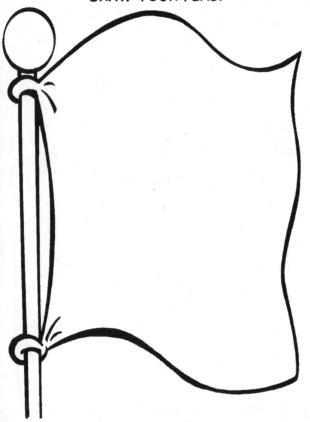

FLYING FRUIT:

THEY TRIED TO LURE THE GORILLA
DOWN WITH AN APPEALING SNACK.
DRAW THE SNACK!

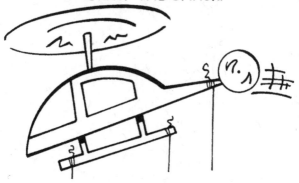

PET PALACE:

DRAW A NEW HOUSE FOR THiS HAMSTER!

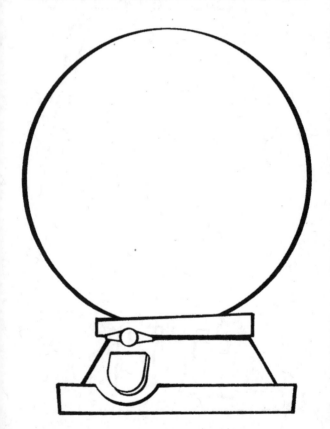

GUM DOODLE:
FILL THIS GUMBALL MACHINE WITH SOMETHING YOU LIKE BETTER THAN GUM!

CANDY DOODLE:
DRAW A CANDY BAR YOU WOULD LOVE TO EAT!

DRAW THE
BOOGIE MAN
(or your weird uncle picking his nose)!

GOOD KNIGHT:

THE KNiGHT iS HOME FROM WORK. DRAW HiS CASTLE!

ART ADDITION 1:

ADD TOGETHER THESE TWO CHARACTERS TO MAKE A THIRD CHARACTER!

ART ADDITION 2:

ADD TOGETHER THESE TWO CHARACTERS TO MAKE A THIRD CHARACTER!

BEAR:
DRAW THE TEDDY BEAR'S FACE
(make him a scary teddy)!

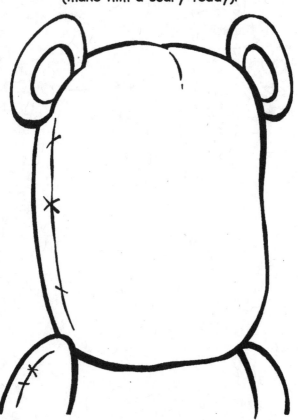

BONES:
DRAW THE SKELETON'S FACE
(make him a friendly skeleton)!

FUTURE FLUSH:
DESIGN THE TOILET OF THE FUTURE!

2-PLY PRESENT:

YOU'VE MADE YOUR MOM A HAT
OUT OF TOILET PAPER. DRAW IT!

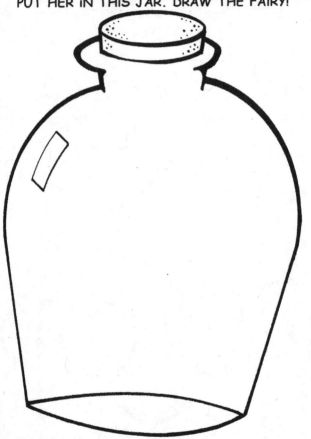

FUMING FAIRY:
YOU'VE CAPTURED THE TOOTH FAIRY AND PUT HER IN THIS JAR. DRAW THE FAIRY!

FIERY FROST:

DRAW JACK FROST ON HIS SUMMER VACATION!

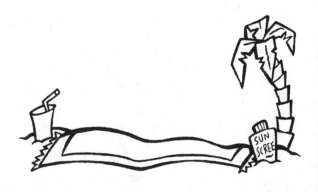

DRAW FRONT:

DRAW THE FRONT OF THE ELEPHANT!

DRAW BACK:
DRAW THE BACK OF THE GiRAFFE!

FOUL:

DRAW WHAT THE NUTTY PITCHER THREW
AT THE BATTER INSTEAD OF A BALL!

PUKE PARK:
DRAW ALL THE PEOPLE GETTING SICK ON THIS ROLLER COASTER!

CRAZY-GO-ROUND:

ON THIS CRAZY CAROUSEL, KIDS DON'T RIDE ON HORSES, BUT SOMETHING TOTALLY DIFFERENT. DRAW IT!

THRILL TOON:

DESiGN AND DRAW THE NEWEST
STOMACH-TURNiNG, BRAiN-WARPiNG
AMUSEMENT-PARK RiDÉ (banned in 7 states)!

OUTSIDE:

MAKE THE OUTSIDE OF YOUR LOCKER LOOK COOL!

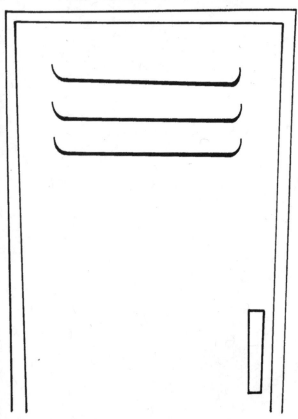

INSIDE:
DRAW WHAT'S INSIDE YOUR BACKPACK!

FISH TAIL:

WHAT DID THE FISH CATCH? DRAW IT!

DESIGN-A-PAD:

DRAW THE MOST AWESOME TREEHOUSE YOU'D LIKE TO LIVE IN!

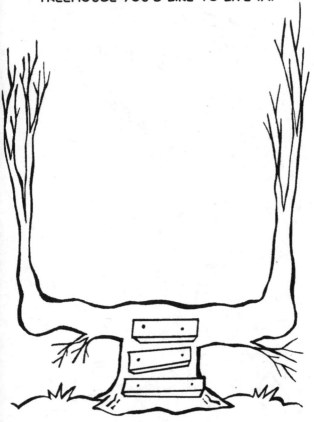

DESIGN-A-DROID:

DRAW THE COOLEST ROBOT
THAT ONLY YOU CAN CONTROL!

STRANGE STRINGS:
DRAW THE WEIRDEST PUPPET EVER!

BOX OF SHOCK:

THIS JACK-IN-THE-BOX IS HAUNTED. DRAW WHAT POPS OUT!

DRAW DRY:

DRAW SOMETHING THAT DOESN'T BELONG IN THIS HOT DESERT!

DRAW DAMP.

DRAW THE REST OF
THIS SUBMARINE!

MARTIAN AUTOPSY:
DRAW THE ALIEN'S iNSiDES!

TOON-ZILLA:

YOUR BIGGEST FEAR IS ATTACKING YOUR TOWN. DRAW IT!

BOYS ON THE MENU:
DRAW THE WILD ANIMAL THAT'S ABOUT TO EAT THESE SCOUTS!

HOW TO MAKE FIRE:

JUST DRAW iT. THE OTHER
WAY TAKES TOO LONG!

YOUR NOSE:

BiLLY BOOGER LiVES iN YOUR NOSE. DRAW HiM AND HiS SiSTER, SNOTTY SALLY!

NO PiCKiNG

EXiT

SNEEZE ZONE

EVIL TWIN:

DRAW WHAT YOUR EVIL
TWIN WOULD LOOK LIKE!

WIZ-ART:

YOU HAVE TO PEE REALLY, REALLY BAD AND THERE'S NO RESTROOM IN SIGHT. DRAW YOUR FACE!

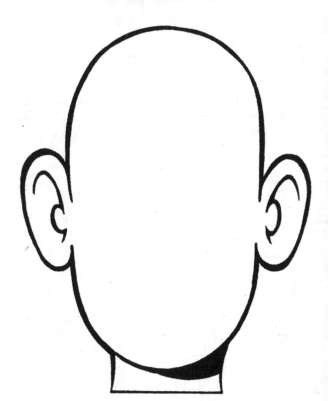

PET WARS 2:

FiDO THREW FLUFFY iNTO THE CLOTHES DRYER. DRAW FLUFFY'S WILD RiDE!

WHEELS:
DRAW AN AWESOME DESIGN ON THE
BOTTOM OF YOUR SKATEBOARD!

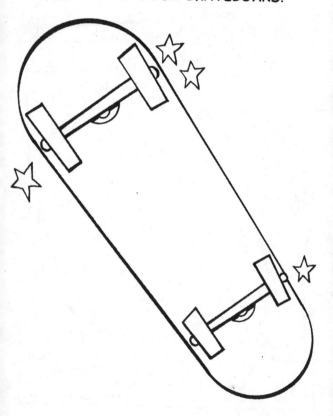

WATER:
DRAW SCARY FISH IN THIS FISH TANK!

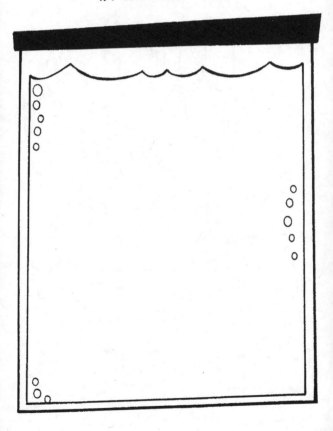

PANIC PICNIC:
DRAW LOTS AND LOTS OF ANTS!

PARK ART:

DRAW THE AMAZING THiNG THESE KiDS HAVE MADE OUT OF SAND!

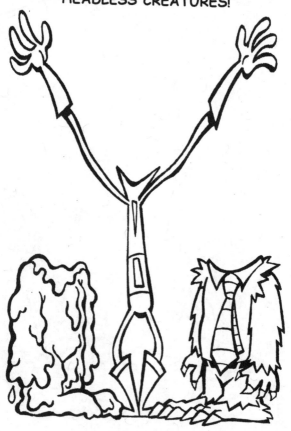

HORRIBLE HEADS:

DRAW HAIR ON THESE STRANGE BALD MEN!

SPORTS GENIE:

THERE'S A GENIE IN THIS KID'S
SPORTS DRINK BOTTLE. DRAW IT!

BURP FAIRY:

DRAW THE BURP FAIRY!

ACHOO!

THE KID BEHIND YOU IN SCIENCE CLASS SNEEZED ALL OVER THE BACK OF YOUR HEAD. DRAW WHAT CAME OUT!

GOO:

YOU'VE CAPTURED ONE OF HiS COLD GERMS AND PUT iT UNDER THE MiCROSCOPE. DRAW iT!

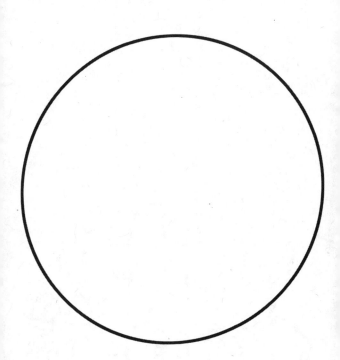

DOGGIE-DOODLE:

DRAW A DOG THAT LOOKS LIKE YOU!

ROBO-DOODLE:

DRAW A ROBOT CAT CHASING THIS ROBOT MOUSE!

POOL PARTY:
DRAW THIS KID SOME FRIENDS!

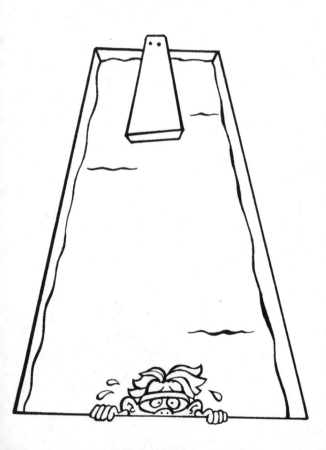

BELLY FLOP:

DRAW YOURSELF DOING A CRAZY DIVE iNTO THE POOL!

MATURE:
DRAW HOW THiS BOY WOULD LOOK AS A GROWN-UP!

MUTATE:

DRAW THIS BABY ALIEN ALL GROWN
UP AND READY TO INVADE EARTH!

LUNCH:

DRAW WHAT (OR WHO)
THE SHARK iS EATiNG!

LEFTOVERS:

DRAW WHAT (OR WHO) THE
ELEPHANT JUST SQUASHED!

SUPERHERO:

DRAW YOURSELF AS A SUPERHERO
WiTH REALLY COOL POWERS!

SIDEKICK:

DRAW ONE OF YOUR FRIENDS, PETS
OR SiBLiNGS AS YOUR LOYAL SiDEKiCK!

SUPERVILLAIN:

CREATE A VILLAIN THAT WILL
BE YOUR SUPER ARCHENEMY!

COMIC COVER:

DESIGN A COMIC BOOK COVER
FEATURING SUPER YOU, YOUR
SIDEKICK AND YOUR ARCHENEMY!

SUPER AWESOME EPIC BATTLE:

ILLUSTRATE THE COOLEST ACTION-
PACKED BATTLE EVER: SUPER YOU & YOUR
SIDEKICK AGAINST YOUR ARCHENEMY!

IT'S SURPRISINGLY RAINING CATS AND DOGS:
DRAW THEM!

IT'S PAINFULLY RAINING

PIGS AND PORCUPINES:

DRAW THEM!

SENIOR:

DRAW HOW YOU'LL LOOK AT YOUR HIGH-SCHOOL GRADUATION!

REALLY SENIOR:

DRAW HOW YOU'LL LOOK
WHEN YOU'RE 300 YEARS OLD!

TAR:

DINOSAURS ARE HAVING A PARTY IN THIS TAR PIT. DRAW THEM!

FEATHER:

DRAW SOME FEATHERS
ON THIS NAKED BIRD!

BRAIN FLUID:

MATH CLASS MELTED THIS KID'S BRAIN.
DRAW iT FLOWiNG OUT OF HiS EAR!

SPITTING IMAGE:

THIS BOY CAN SPIT IN ANY SHAPE.
DRAW HIS SPIT ART!

SLEEPWALKER:

DRAW THE WEIRD PLACE THIS SLEEPWALKER ENDED UP!

SLEEP COUNTER:

THIS KID HATES SHEEP. DRAW WHAT HE'S COUNTING TO FALL ASLEEP!

CAR TOON:

DESIGN AND DRAW A
FLYING CAR OF THE FUTURE!

CARTOON:

YOU ARE NOW OFFICIALLY A CARTOONIST.
DRAW A CARTOON HERE!

POCKET:

DRAW THE DOODLES ON THE COVER OF
POCKETDOODLES FOR BUGS!

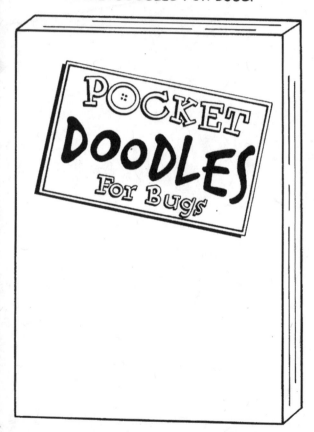

DOODLES:
NOW CREATE YOUR OWN COVER!

FINISH:

DRAW YOUR FACE (AND HAIR) ON THE LAST DAY OF SCHOOL!

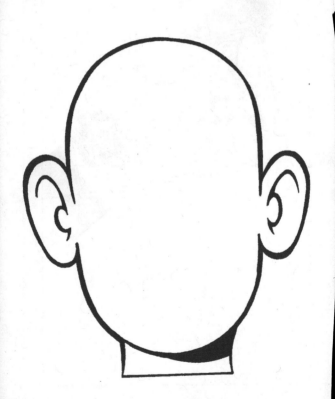